COINS OF THE ANARCHY 1135—54

By Geor

NATIONAL MUSEUM OF WALES
AMGUEDDFA GENEDLAETHOL CYMRU

in association with

A.H. BALDWIN & SONS LTD.
11 Adelphi Terrace, London WC2

First published in 1988

© National Museum of Wales,
 Cathays Park, Cardiff

Production: Hywel G. Rees
Typesetting: Afal, Cardiff
Type: Baskerville 11/12 pt
Photography: Eric Broadbent
Artwork: Studio 1, Caerphilly
Paper: Ikonolux 135 gsm
Printing: South Western Printers, Caerphilly

ISBN: 0 7200 0325 3

Front cover: *Penny of Maud, Wenallt hoard (no. 9)*
Back cover: *Ladies of the twelfth century, wearing kerchiefs.*
 From Strutt's Dresses, *1799, after MS illustrations*

Foreword

In November 1980, a hoard of over 100 silver pennies, found the previous June at Coed-y-Wenallt overlooking Cardiff, was declared Treasure Trove at a Coroner's Inquest, and was subsequently valued at £103,040. The Museum bought 34 of the coins and in 1987 through Messrs. Spink & Son added an unrecorded stray. Why should these little, ill-struck, brittle discs claim such a high valuation?

The find was sensational. The Wenallt hoard trebled at a stroke the known coins of the Empress Maud, who in the 1140s disputed the throne of England with her cousin, Stephen; it was largely composed of coins of Cardiff mint, hitherto extremely rare, besides adding the name of a baron, John of St. John, to the numismatic record; it added for good measure the first-known coins of a Swansea mint, including some in the name of another baron, Henry de Neubourg; and in short it added substantially to the record of those troubled times.

As part of its collecting-policy, the Museum already had a small series of coins of the period; but this unexpected addition has encouraged a specialization which has made the Welsh public owners of many interesting, rare, and even unique coins. The author of this picture book, now Curator of the Museum's main building in Cathays Park, had the singular good fortune to have the handling of the Wenallt find, and to shape the collection as a whole. Here he presents the results so far.

D. W. Dykes,
Director *November 1988*

Conflict

Maud or Matilda was designated by Henry I as his heir. His son William had been drowned at sea; Robert Earl of Gloucester and Lord of Glamorgan — Robert 'the Consul' as he liked to be known — was Henry's eldest son, but was illegitimate. Maud alone was left *a legali conjuge*, and more than once the barons had been made by Henry to swear allegiance to her. As a girl, she had been married off to the German Emperor, Henry V, who died childless in 1125; and though she was again married, three years later, to Geoffrey the Handsome, Count of Anjou, in furtherance of her father's schemes, she kept the title of Empress. In 1133, she bore a son destined to become England's Henry II (see p.7).

Like Maud, Stephen was a grandchild of the Conqueror, and by marriage became Count of Boulogne. He was brave, swift to action, and of an astonishing simplicity of manner. On Henry I's death at Rouen in December 1135, he rushed to London, secured the support of the influential business-community, seized the royal treasury at Winchester, and was crowned (according to William of Malmesbury) on Sunday, December 22. All this was done with the help of his brother Henry, Bishop of Winchester, Abbot of Glastonbury and Papal Legate. Little was so far heard of Maud; but in 1137 Stephen, already no stranger to a catastrophe in Wales, an invasion of northern England by the Scots, and a rebellion in Devon, was faced with a serious situation in Normandy. He left the Justiciar, Roger Bishop of Salisbury in charge of the kingdom; but as a Henry I man Roger favoured the legitimate heir, and

Pfennig of the Emperor Henry V, crowned 1111, died 1125. The other side shows SS Simon and Jude. Struck at Goslar. By permission of the Trustees of the British Museum.

actually issued coins bearing the Empress's title (no.10). Even more important, having been the victim of a clumsy assassination attempt, the Consul renounced his allegiance in 1138, and remained until his death in 1147 an unswerving supporter of his half-sister.

Maud landed near Arundel in September 1139; and with the quixotic temperament uniquely his, Stephen sent her under safe-conduct to Bristol, where the Consul's headquarters were. Civil war soon became general, for the barons were divided. Both the Consul and his son-in-law, Ranulf Earl of Chester, could count on raising large numbers of Welsh mercenaries to offset Stephen's Flemish mercenaries deployed under William of Ypres. A great battle outside Lincoln in February 1141 resulted in Stephen's capture.

Maud made her exultant way to Winchester, where in April a council summoned by Bishop Henry, as Papal Legate, declared her *Domina*

COINS OF THE ANARCHY 1135—54

supplied by
Spin-A-Disc
Promotions

107, KEIGHLEY ROAD, ILLINGWORTH,
HALIFAX, WEST YORKSHIRE HX2 8JE
Tel. (0422) 245401

Marriage-feast of Maud and the Emperor Henry V at Mainz, 1114. From an anonymous chronicle belonging to the Empress. Copyright Corpus Christi College, Cambridge (MS 373). With the earliest representation of a pretzel?

Anglorum — 'Lady of the English' — and so, with no other claimant in sight, the feudal overlord of all the baronage. Arrangements were made for her coronation at Westminster. However, Maud's arrogant disposition and harsh demands, joined with the knowledge that Stephen's queen, also Matilda and equally redoubtable (cf.no.35), was marching through Kent towards London at the head of a mercenary army, lent the Londoners courage to drive the Empress away. The Maudian high summer was therefore brief. Winchester, of all places, was unsafe; and her withdrawal from the city became a rout in September. The Consul was taken prisoner; but Maud under the protection of her greatest favourite and likely lover, Brien fitz Count, Lord of Wallingford (no.24), escaped to the west. Both parties thus reverted to their positions of two years before. There was an exciting escape for Maud, from snowbound Oxford all dressed in white when, in 1142, she again sought sanctuary with Brien; but gradually she withdrew from active participation in the sporadic campaigning which was devastating as much as a third of the productive land at the interface between the Maudian south and west and the royalist remainder of the kingdom. Early in 1148, after Robert the Consul's death, she retired to Rouen; she was still only 46, and lived for almost another twenty years, respected by all, and dying a nun.

Her son Henry of Anjou, 'fitz Empress,' visited England as a small boy; in 1147 (when Stephen kindly returned the young paladin); and in 1149, when he was sixteen, and together with his friend Roger Earl of Hereford was ready to be knighted by his uncle David, King of Scots, still firmly in occupation of Carlisle. In 1153, Henry returned again, a very different figure: he had been invested with the Duchy of Normandy by his father (who had captured it in 1144); by Geoffrey's death he was Count of Anjou; and by marriage with the experienced Eleanor of Aquitaine held the dukedom of that region too, not to mention Maine. He conducted a soldierly campaign through the western borderlands, and a truce with Stephen at Wallingford led, with the support of the barons, to a peace-treaty at Winchester (promulgated later at Westminster) which safeguarded Stephen's throne but recognised Henry as his heir: Eustace, Stephen's elder son, whose succession the king had vainly been trying to encompass, had very recently died; the queen had died in 1152; and William, the younger son, was still a boy for whom good provision could be and was made. Even Stephen himself did not long survive this crisis; he died in his fifties (October 24, 1154). Henry, away in Normandy, saw no reason to rush to England. His coronation took place at Westminster on December 19.

8

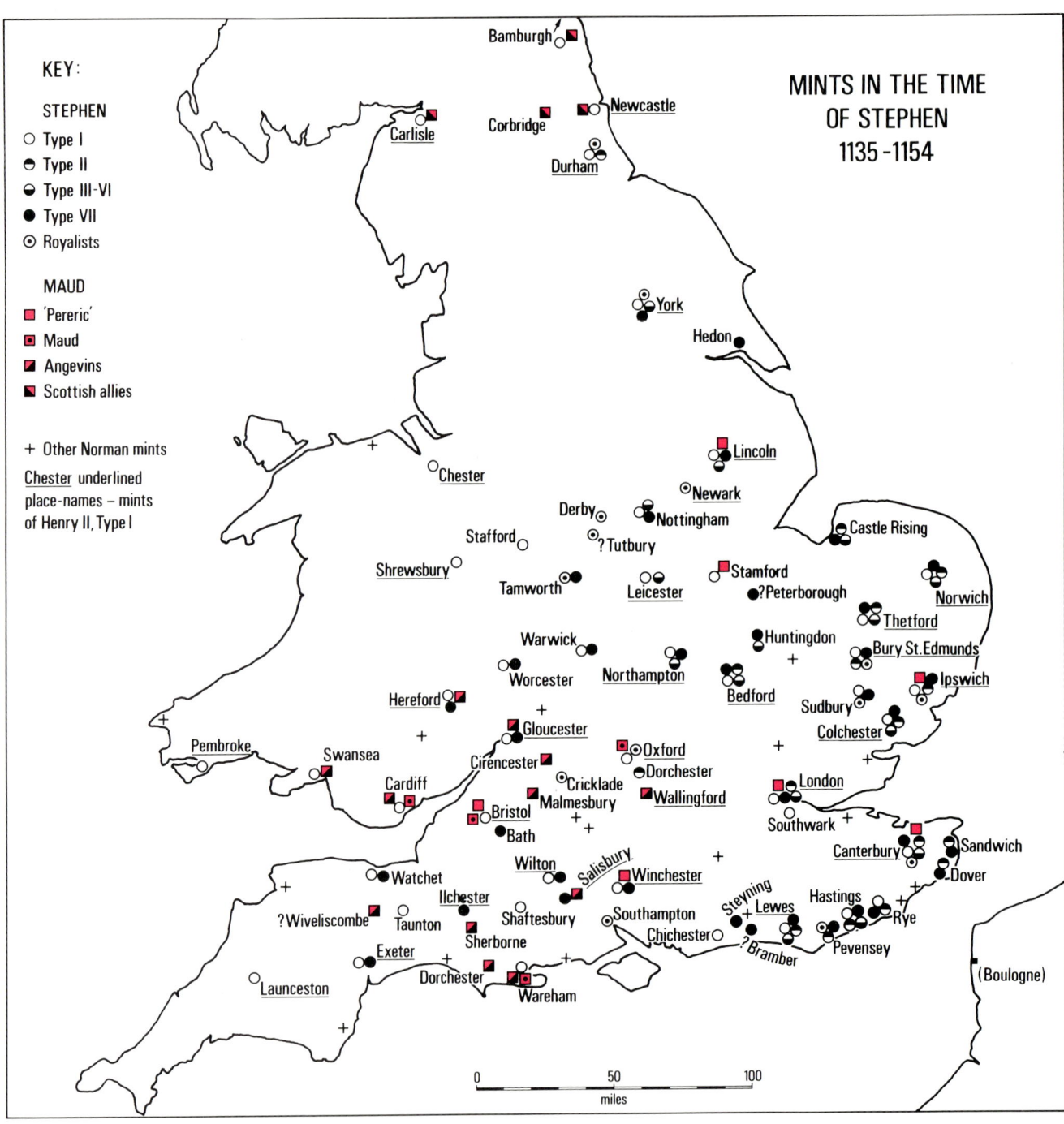

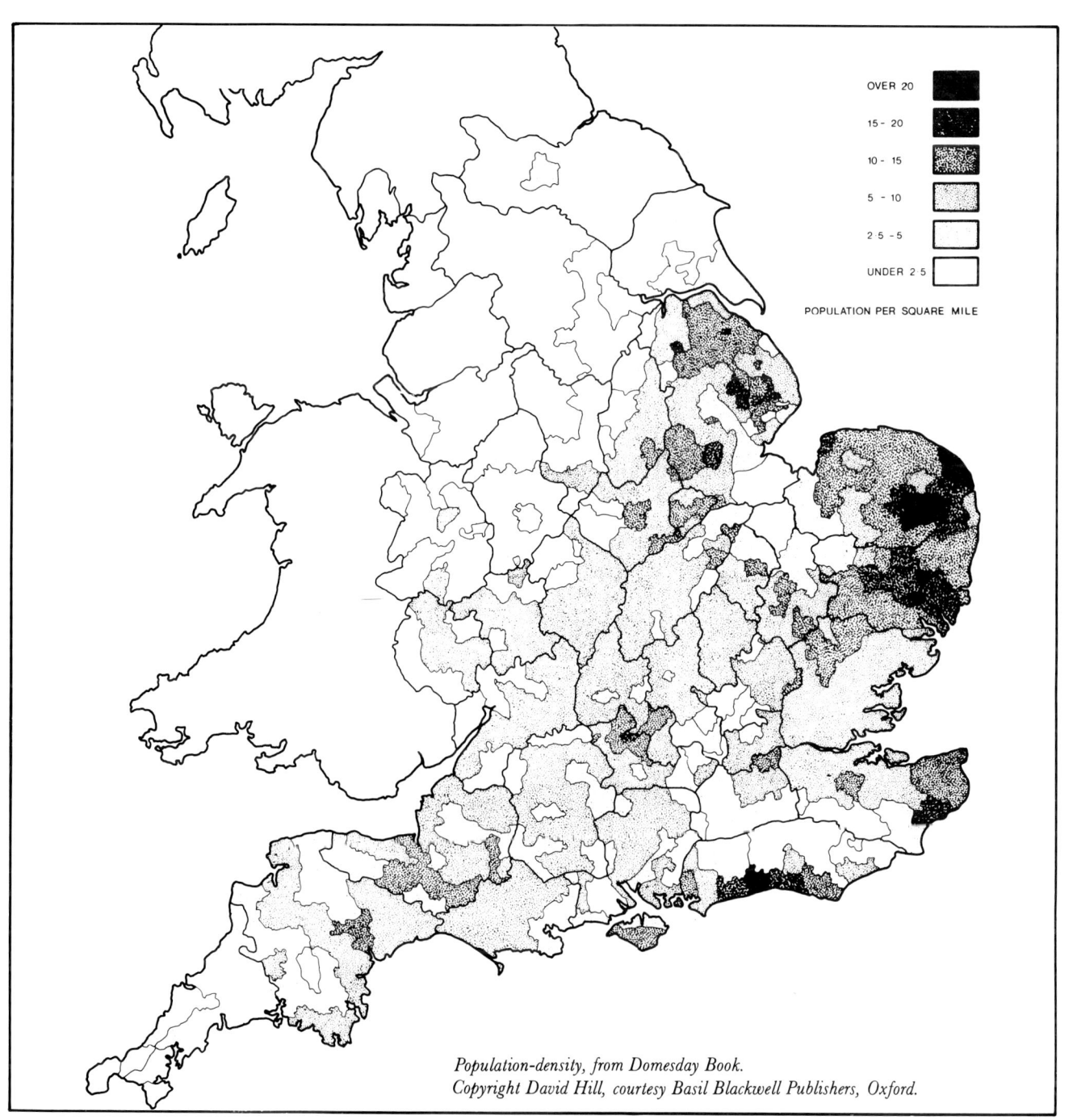

Population-density, from Domesday Book.
Copyright David Hill, courtesy Basil Blackwell Publishers, Oxford.

The Coinage

The only coin was the silver penny, issued in boroughs — walled towns — up and down the land: some 45 for Stephen's first issue, about average for the period, though Henry I's last type had been struck at only 20. The boroughs were named on the coins, as also were the responsible moneyers. These were substantial merchants or officials, employing their own staff in their own premises, or in shared accommodation. Unlike the system on the Continent, where the right of coinage was very widely, indeed minutely, dispersed, moneyers in England seem to have been under contract with the Crown and were strictly controlled, even though a borough or a lord, lay or ecclesiastical, might enjoy profits from the services of a moneyer or might even possess a right of mintage under the Crown. Stephen's reign saw the royal prerogative challenged — not by Maud, a rival, but apparently by barons. The appearance of their names on certain coins retaining a royal bust is a question to be examined (p.29). The status of mints varied according to the vitality of trade — trade that brought the bullion, for local production except at Alston, near Carlisle, was unimportant. A town with a flourishing trade might have several moneyers — there were eight at London — and a tiny place like Pembroke might have only one. The system had operated with some success since its introduction by Æthelstan about 935.

The coins are crude: the scratchy lettering on Maud's, imperfectly imprinted from the dies, was not puzzled out until 1851, when (Sir) John Evans published a specimen; and even in 1980, it was some time before the barbarous Swansea pieces in the Wenallt hoard yielded their secrets to patient study. The reason is that the silver sheet was not properly annealed, or was of varying thickness, or when stamped out with a ring-punch the edges were badly buckled; mainly, however, the uneven impression arose because the upper die was not held perfectly upright. In such troubled times, indeed, a man might well attempt to conceal his authorship by slightly tilting the die. No.17 is perhaps an example.

Pepys observed of the new coins of Charles II that it was 'strange to see how good they are in the stamp and bad in the money, for lack of skill to make them'; and this is a comment which applies to the Norman coinage too, when the fitz Ottos — the king's goldsmiths who had held the monopoly of die-cutting since the Conquest — continued the practice begun under the Confessor and Harold of providing not merely the image of the king, but an individual characterization. This, despite the tiny scale and the caricaturing unavoidable at busy periods, it may not be wrong to call a portrait (nos.2-8); other representations (as no.1) are still more concerned with the kingly status. The large scope of royal seals offered an easier field to the artist, who may have worked from sketches taken from the life; perhaps seals were the proximal source for the die-cutter. Even in the case of Maud (no.9), however, a local engraver achieved a distinct characterization for the Cardiff Class A dies; others at Bristol, Oxford and Wareham may perhaps have been imitations, rough at that.

To the modern mind, the strangest feature of the late Saxon and Norman coinage is the periodical change of design. Some types have a profile portrait, others a full-face; and there is a great variety of the cruciform patterns on the reverses. The purpose of the change was fiscal, for the moneyers had then to pay for their dies, usually 20 shillings, and another 20 shillings after a short interval to the king, or other proprietor of the mint: at Hereford, the Bishop had one of the moneyers and so claimed his 20 shillings, as *Domesday Book* relates. The Crown also received fines levied for the continuing use of obsolete dies, which had to be defaced and returned to the Exchequer (cf.no.13). We have record that in 1130 Gillapatric, the Pembroke moneyer, was subject to a forfeit of £4 on this account, but had paid £2 of it.

Since the penny was the only coin, vast numbers were accumulated. The cash seized by Stephen at Winchester in 1135 comprised £100,000 of *exquisitissimi denarii* — 'very carefully chosen pence' — 24,000,000 coins; and when Bishop Roger, disgraced, stacked the residue of his fortune on the high altar of Salisbury Cathedral as a gift towards its completion, it amounted to 80,000 marks, or 12,800,000 coins (the mark, 13s.4d., was a widely-used unit-of-account). These vast mintages, treasured up, have long since gone back to the melting-pot: the bullion was recycled again and again. The largest Norman hoard ever brought to light was at Beauworth near Winchester, in 1833: it consisted of only 8,000 pence, though that would have been a fortune to the ordinary wage-earner, at a time when a penny-a-day was the basic figure. It was necessary to provide halfpence and farthings by cutting pennies, using the reverse cross as a guide. Examples of not much later date, from the Towy shore at Llanstephan, tell us what the ferryman's fee was, for both foot-passengers and horsemen. The cutting was supposed to be done at the mint; but who was to tell if a sliver fell to one side, then

Obverse die for a penny of Stephen. It would have been fixed in a block of wood.
The blank placed on top would have been imprinted by the hand-held upper die, struck by a workman.
Copyright, Museum of London.

Romanesque capital at the church of Saint-Georges-de-Boscherville, Normandy, showing a workman (St. Eloi) holding hammer and upper die; the lower die is shown at his side, set in a block of wood. Coins were normally struck by a seated workman. Copyright, Administration des Monnaies et Médailles, Paris.

or subsequently? It was a wise provision, in the *Law of Hywel*, for a cut halfpenny to be reckoned at three to a penny, not two.

The moneyer's name on the reverse of every penny stood as a commitment to due standards of weight and fineness — a guarantee to king, lord and public. The weight of the penny averaged 20.4, say $20\frac{1}{2}$, grains ('of wheat from the midst of the ear'), 1.39 grammes; but wartime coins often fell far short of this figure, even though the quality of their silver was excellent. Counting in the residual gold and lead, as the medieval assayer would have done without realising, the fineness of 20 pennies non-destructively analysed by J.P.Northover averages 93.9%. It is worth remark that in 1279, when a total reform of the coinage was undertaken by Edward I, it was pointed out that the old coin collected for melting might very well turn out to be better than sterling (92.5%).

The lightweight wartime and particularly the Angevin coins are interesting from an unexpected point of view, for their presence in the purses of returning Welsh mercenaries, sutlers and traders — such a man hid the Wenallt hoard just over the border into Welsh Senghenydd from Norman Cardiff — may explain a conundrum of the *Law of Hywel*, the earliest texts of which are of the 13th century, after our period, even though Hywel Dda himself died in 950. Among the graduated fines and valuations, we find reference to two kinds of penny, 'legal' (*kyfreith*) and 'short' (*cota*). For us it is difficult to grasp that there was no relationship: each was equally a penny, or 'image' (*delu*), to the Welshman. Thus, a draught ox increased in value season by season up to 60 pence, four of which were 'short' but are counted in this total. The pennies of the Anarchy can alone answer to this curious category.

Schedule

NOTE

Illegible letters in square brackets — weight in grammes — angle of reverse to obverse (die-axis) in degrees — fineness inclusive, per cent. — E-number, the catalogue-number — sales by collector's name, date, and lot (in brackets).
The moneyers' names, erratically spelt, are given in proper form; some place-names are abbreviated on the coins.

All coins are illustrated twice actual size (two diameters)

NORMAN PORTRAITS

1. **William the Conqueror, 1066-1087, Type VI**

   +PILLELM REX I *crowned facing bust holding sword of state*
   +EDPI ON LVNDNE *cross pattée on quadrilateral treflé*
   1.34 g. 180°. E.759. Bought Baldwin, 1978.

The apparent P is the Old English form of W, and the I is not a numeral but the first leg of the A of *Anglorum* ('of the English'), there not being room for more. The moneyer is Eadwig 'at London' (ON being Old English for 'at'). His is a Saxon name and shows with a multitude of others that the Conquest, though upsetting the landowning ranks of society, scarcely interfered with the merchant class. Nor was there any change to the coinage, apart from design, until 1158 when the periodical changes were stopped.

The portrait is derived from King William's seal and emphasizes the continuity of the monarchy; even the crown resembles one on Saxon coins, though there is a considerable variety at this period. The moustache is worth noting (cf. also no.2): on the Bayeux Tapestry the Normans are clean-shaven, and it is the Saxons (and Count Eustace of Boulogne) who wear moustaches. Indeed the *Roman de Rou* tells of an English spy sent by Harold who reported that the Norman army consisted only of priests *'Kar tuit erent tonduz e rez / Ne lor esteit guernon remez,'* 'For all were shorn and shaved / Nor was moustache them saved.' Ranulf, Earl of Chester in Maud's time, was still unusual in wearing a moustache and accordingly had the nickname 'de Gernons'. The adoption of the Saxon fashion by King William and his son may perhaps be another mark of intentional assimilation.

William I Type III, moneyer Siboda at London. It shows the royal bust under a 'canopy' representing the audience-hall. E.754. Bt. Baldwin.

Type III represents the majesty of kingship even better than Type VI, for there the bust is framed by a canopy-like structure which represents a royal audience-hall in a convention going back to late Antiquity. Several appear on the Bayeux Tapestry, William's in Scene 48 (Wilson) being quite close to this. But Type VI is chosen because the earliest Norman penny from Wales, indeed from Cardiff Castle, is of that type and is doubtless related to the Conqueror's St. David's expedition of 1081. The 'building' of Cardiff town is assigned in the *Annales de Margan* to that year, and William would have left

1

2

3

4

5

6

a strong force behind at his bridgehead on the Welsh side of the Bristol Channel. The choice of site probably fell on Cardiff because the defences of the old Roman fort could be refurbished and the position strengthened by a timber-built castle standing on a huge mound thrown up within the enclosure. Men-at-arms and workmen would have needed pay, and this coin (which is from locally-cut dies) seems to have been struck by 'Hervé at Cardiff' — the earliest coin struck in Wales. The link with the expedition of 1081 would also provide the only direct evidence as to the date when Type VI was actually current.

William I Type VI, moneyer Hervé at Cardiff. The earliest Norman coin struck in Wales, found at Cardiff Castle, gift of the Marquess of Bute. Drawn by Colin Williams. E760.

William and advisers in an audience-hall, on the eve of the Battle of Hastings. Bayeux Tapestry. By special permission, la Ville de Bayeux.

2. William Rufus, 1087-1100, Type I

    + PILLELM REX I *crowned profile bust holding sword, right*
    +IERNEPI ON SCRVBS *cross pattée on saltire fleury*
    1.29 g. 360°. E.800. Bought Mack II Sale, 1977 (244).

'Earnwig at *Scrubbesbyrig*' — the 'borough amid the scrub', Shrewsbury, a mint from Æthelstan onwards, and in 1071 the seat of Roger de Montgomery, one of the three magnates to whom William I had entrusted the security of the Welsh borders, the *Marchia Walliae*; Roger was also to found Montgomery itself, giving it his name.

On this coin note the rugged features and a head more rounded than his father's. This coin was probably struck about 1090-3: the only variety of William II's datable by historical context is Type II, of which a unique coin again from local dies, now in the British Museum, was minted at Rhyd-y-gors (Carmarthen) during the first brief Norman occupation (1093-6) by William fitz Baldwin. There is an electrotype of that coin in the National Museum.

3. Henry I, 1100-1135, Type XI

+hENR RE crowned profile bust holding sceptre, left
+PALTERVS · O/ +N · CARDII: in two rings, central cross
l.29 g. 360°. 94.1%. E.838/2. From the Llantrithyd (Glam.) hoard of 8 Type XI pennies, 1962-3, given by the Friends of the National Museum of Wales.

'Walter at Cardiff'. The king's face is very different from his brother's: longer, with large eyes, and luxuriant hair swept back — a French royal fashion (as on the seal, p.41) which the Church regarded as thoroughly effeminate; Ordericus Vitalis tells how the aged Bishop of Séez preached an impassioned sermon on the point and, pulling out a pair of shears, cut off the offending locks of King Henry and all his courtiers.

Notice the small cut in the edge about 9 o'clock on the obverse: all pennies had to be snicked in this way for some years after 1114 to display their solid silver core. There had been an outbreak of counterfeiting, and apparently the public was so suspicious of all coins which had been tested — even if proved sound — that this curious instruction had to be sent out to all moneyers. Type XI was issued about 1122-4. The acquisition of the Llantrithyd hoard, from the site of a small manor-house in the Vale of Glamorgan, has made the National Museum exceptionally rich in a scarce and handsome variety of 12th-century coin.

4-8. Stephen, 1135-1154, Type I

On the following five coins we note the standardised metropolitan portrait with its long, straight nose rather bulbous at its tip. The lily crown worn by Stephen was used for some of Henry I's coins, but not for any of the Williams', even though the Confessor and Harold are both shown wearing it on the Bayeux Tapestry. Stephen's adoption of it may have been intended to stress his rightful possession of the English throne. On the coin, it lacks the side-pendants depicted on the first seal of the reign. Fancy has claimed that the cross moline and lilies of the reverse design represent a top view of this crown.

It is a numismatic axiom that a title is shortened as time goes by. Thus STIEFNE REX ends as merely STIEFNE (no.8). This last was a stage reached by 1139 after about 3½ years' issue, for there is a Bristol penny with that reading which must be earlier than the Empress's arrival in the town. Likewise no.8 must have appeared before Earl Ranulf went over to the Maudians late in 1140: it is highly unlikely that it was struck as late as 1146, when there was a very brief rapprochement with the king. There has been a notion in recent years that Type I went on to the 1150's in the west, but it rests on misconception.

The boroughs striking pennies of Stephen's Type I (open circles on the map) were tiny by our standards, some having only a local significance as market-centres, though others had developed a flourishing trade, which of course increased with the strengthened links across the English Channel after the Conquest: hence the importance of the south-east coastal mints, where Continental coin was refined and turned into English money. Judging the importance of the towns by their number of moneyers, London and Norwich (for the cloth trade) stand supreme in Stephen's day, Lincoln, Ipswich, Canterbury, Winchester and York trailing behind. It is interesting to compare (pp.8-9) the map of mints with that of the population (based on *Domesday Book*, 1086). 95% of the population was engaged on the land, and town-dwellers too were bound up with the agricultural year; as late as 1338, a London statute laid down that all those practising crafts of which 'a man hath no great need in harvest-time shall be compelled to serve in harvest, to cut, gather and bring in the corn.' In this light, the rapine of the Anarchy years

7

8

9

10

11

12

can be understood, and with it the barons' rejection of continuing warfare when it had become obvious that Henry fitz Empress was the man of the future. The sudden death of Eustace merely confirmed their view.

4. +STIFNE R[E]X *crowned bust holding sceptre right*
   +PILLE[M:]ON:CARDI *cross moline and lilies*
   1.40 g. 360°. 95.23%. E.917. Bought Elmore Jones II Sale, 1984 (1379).

Only four of these pennies by 'Willelm at Cardiff', all from the same dies, are known. The moneyer may be the reeve (lord's steward) of the tiny Cardiff borough, who is recorded about this time. *Stifne* is the earliest spelling, soon becoming *Stiefne* in accordance with a pronunciation which gave a *y*-sound to the *e*, as in 'yes' — *Styefn*'. Robert the Consul, who had married the daughter of fitz Haimo, conqueror of Glamorgan, did homage to Stephen for his lands in April 1136, and this coin will have been struck soon afterwards. In the dark days of the Welsh assault on Gower, William continued to supply coin even though London dies were not available, and the barbarous products of a local die-sinker are well represented in the Wenallt hoard.

5. +STIEFNE [RE]:
   +GIL[PAT]RIC:O[N:P]AN
   1.37 g. 360°. 94.88%. E.906. From Lockett Sale I, 1955 (1108), given by the Lockett family.

Pembroke (*Pan-, Penbroc*) had been founded by Roger de Montgomery in 1093, and after a period in the king's hands it had been granted by Stephen in 1138 to Gilbert de Clare. Gillapatric, an Irishman, had been sole moneyer there since about 1125 (cf.p.11). Only eleven coins have been recorded from his dies, plus another two by another moneyer, Walter, whereon the place-name is abbreviated to PAIN (perhaps a mistake for PAM). They are of Henry II's 'Tealby' type, current from 1158 (cf.no.40); and if the numismatic ordering of that series is correct, are too early for there to have been any connexion with Henry II's visits in 1171-2 to treat with the Lord Rhys, and on his return from Ireland. The National Museum has examples of all the types attributed to Pembroke.

6. +STIEFNE RE:
   +PIHCRIC[:]ON:hEREFO
   1.47 g. 360°. 95.74%. E.918. Bought Elmore Jones II Sale, 1984 (1384).

'Wihtric at Hereford' — another mint which operated under Æthelstan. As early as 1067 Hereford was the seat of William fitz Osbern, another of the three magnates to whom the March of Wales was entrusted.

7. [+]STIEFNE RE:
   +hER[R]EVI:ON:LEPE
   1.42 g. 90°. E.905. From Lockett Sale I, 1955 (1100), given by the Lockett family. From the Watford hoard of 1818.

Out of over 1,000 coins in the Watford hoard, Stephen's Type I accounted for nearly 650, so that it is often called the 'Watford' type. This penny by Hervé at Lewes is chosen to demonstrate the unity of style achieved by the fitz Otto workshop right across the kingdom.

8. +STIEFNE
   +ALME[R:O]N:CES
   1.25 g. 360°. E.920. Bought Spink 1985 from Elmore Jones I Sale, 1983 (431).

This coin by Aymer at Chester is not a particularly good specimen in itself, but does illustrate the shortest obverse legend (p.17).

9. The Empress Maud, Type I / Class A

:[M]ATILLIS:IM[PER] crowned bust holding sceptre, right
[+BRIC]MER:CAIERDI: cross moline and lilies
1.15 g. 90° 93.34%. E.1000/45. From the Coed-y-Wenallt treasure trove, 1980.

'Beorhtmaer, Cardiff'. Great pains were taken, despite the scratchy lettering, to produce a womanly portrait. See above, p.10; and further under no.15. Was she ever at Cardiff, for it to be drawn? The castle had accommodation fit for Robert, Duke of Normandy, who had been under perpetual house-arrest there 1126-1134, so she could have been appropriately received in Wales.

A TROUBLED LAND

The next five coins, issued between 1137 and 1139 (or later, for no.12) illustrate the break-down of royal authority over the coinage. All Type I.

10. *+PERERIC: crowned bust holding sceptre, right*
+GODRIC[VS]:ON:LV cross moline and lilies
143 g. 45°. E.972. Bought Spink 20th Sale, 1982 (92). From the Linton (Maidstone) hoard, 1883.

The obverse invites comparison with the Anglo-Norman word *Emperériz* (Empress), and a few dies even have a terminal M. It would be far too great a coincidence if there had been no connexion with Maud; however, the coins come from mints which, save for Bristol, she never controlled (open red squares on the map), and the dies are metropolitan — as in this case, struck by 'Godric at London.' The issue is therefore prewar, as indeed the good weight of the coins suggests. Marion Archibald has suggested that it was probably produced on the orders of Roger, Bishop of Salisbury, Justiciar of England appointed by Henry I, in 1137; Stephen, then in Normandy, was faced with serious unrest, an Angevin invasion, and the disintegration of his forces. As a Maudian sympathiser, Roger may have chanced his hand; but Stephen survived, and in 1139 deprived him of power and possessions.

11. *+S[TI]EFNE REIS*
+EINI ON ESWENSI
1.00 g. 45°. E. 1000/19. From the Coed-y-Wenallt treasure trove, 1980.

Swansea had never possessed a mint, though it was *caput* of the Lordship of Gower (quite separate from the Lordship of Glamorgan) from 1116, when Henry, first Earl of Warwick, conquered the region. This is from the first issue — obviously from local dies cut by a very unskilled hand, obviously to meet an emergency demand for cash — probably to pay for men-at-arms or supplies, for Swansea never fell to the Welsh onslaught of 1136 though most of Gower was retaken. This penny must have been struck on the order of the Earl's younger son, Henry de Neubourg, between 1137 and 1140, when the Earl went over to the Empress (see further, no.23).

It is an interesting coin: the use of the Anglo-Norman *reis* for *rex* is paralleled by *erl* instead of *comes* (earl) on no.12. On the other side, the moneyer cannot have been *Eini(on)*, a Welshman, in the circumstances: the name is *Henri* miscut; again, that cannot be Henry de Neubourg, but a merchant or official, for a baron would not take on such a rôle.

This coin gives us the earliest form of Swansea's name (with euphonic initial E): all the early forms give *Swen-* rather than *Swan-*, which does not appear until 1291, in the *Taxatio Ecclesiastica*. Until the Wenallt hoard came to light, the earliest mention of *Sweynesse* occurred in a copy, made under Edward I, of the borough's first charter granted by the third Earl of Warwick between 1153 and 1184.

13

14

15

16

17

18

12. *[+h]ENRIC ERL ·*
    +EREBALD · ON[· CO]RE
    1.21 g. 180°. E.990. Bought Spink, 1982 as a recent north-country find.

'Herebald at *Corebricg* (Corbridge-on-Tyne)'. Maud's uncle, David King of Scots, who had invaded northern England in 1136 in support of her cause, was decisively defeated in the 'Battle of the Standard' near Northallerton in 1138; in the settlement, however, Stephen created David's son Henry Earl of Northumbria. Prince Henry died in 1152, but from 1136 to 1157 the whole northern part of the kingdom was in Scottish hands. Herebald had originally been Stephen's moneyer, briefly, at Carlisle, and continued to strike there for David. See further, no.40.

Edward the Confessor Type V, moneyer Leofstan at Canterbury. From a cancelled obverse die (note bar across the sceptre). E.656.

13. *+STIEFNE:R:*
    +SPIEN:ON:SNOT
    0.94 g. 270°. E.953. Bought Spink 20th Sale, 1982 (93). From the Nottingham hoard, 1880 though provenance in the sale-catalogue is wrong.

'Sveinn at *Snotingeham* (Nottingham)'. The appearance of this coin is due to its having been struck from worn-out dies. A crack in the obverse die shows as a vertical ridge on the left, the die itself having been cancelled by the moneyer, who cut an oblique cross over the king's face, and engraved a big pellet just beneath (see p.11). If the Nottingham hoard was concealed before the great fire of 1140 as has generally been agreed, the coins cannot be connected with the Papal interdict of 1148, as has recently been argued; and another fire in 1153 does not much help. The interest of the piece lies in its testimony to the total breakdown of normal die-replacement arising from the war. Various other mints used cancelled dies, each having its characteristic mode of cancellation; occasionally cancelled dies were in emergency use at other periods, and the National Museum collection includes a Canterbury penny of the Confessor with a cancellation-bar across the sceptre.

14. *[+]S[TIEFNE R:]*
    [+G]VRDAN[:ON]: BR[I]S:
    1.31 g. 180°. 96.61%. E.951. Bought Baldwin, 1978 from the Hanham and Wells collections; cast in the British Museum.

'Jordan at Bristol' — he was probably a Jewish merchant. Here the obverse die has not merely been cancelled but thoroughly defaced and obliterated, except for the ghost of the S. This must have been done very soon after the arrival of the Empress in September, 1139.

COINS OF THE EMPRESS AND THE ANGEVIN CAUSE

The Empress's name appears on coins from only a few mints. Two, Cardiff and Bristol, were the capitals of her half-brother Robert's honours of Glamorgan and Gloucester. A third, Wareham, was for much of the period the chief Angevin entrepôt for the western parts of the realm in their hands. A fourth, at Oxford, probably coined only briefly for her. A fifth is unidentified and is therefore not shown on the map among the red squares with central dot. Nos.15-18, Type I.

Impression of the Empress's one-sided seal, naming her only as Queen of the Romans. Full size.

15. :M[AT]ILLIS:IM[P]ER *crowned bust holding sceptre, right*
[+BRI]CMER:CAIER[DI] *cross moline and lilies*
0.82 g. 360°. E. 1000/46. From the Coed-y-Wenallt treasure trove, 1980.

This is from the same dies as no.9. The weight-range of the suite of 33 pennies from these dies, represented in the hoard, was 1.14 down to 0.64 grammes, so illustrating the very unsatisfactory control over weight at the Cardiff mint of the time. The silver, however, remained good.

16. :MATILD[I] IN:
| [T]V[RChIL:]O[N]: BRI:
1.25 g. 20°. E.1000/26. From the Coed-y-Wenallt treasure trove, 1980.

'Thorketill at Bristol' was one of three moneyers who had struck for Stephen before the Empress's arrival. Coins from the same pair of dies in the Ashmolean Museum and in the Prestwich (Manchester) hoard of 1972 clarify the poorly-imprinted reverse legend.

17. :MA[TILDI IMP]:
[+RAVL · DE] · WAR · HA[M]
0.94 g. 270°. E.981. Bought Baldwin, 1978, from the Hanham collection.

Raulf's Wareham penny retains just enough to show that it is a die-duplicate of another, enabling the legend to be restored. He may have fled when Stephen took the town in 1142; a Bristol penny of Wenallt Class B (see no.19) seems to bear his name, but is badly double-struck.

18. :[M]ATILDI:I[MP·]
+SWET[IN]G:ON:OX:
1.07 g. 90°. 89.49%. E.980. Bought Spink 1st Sale, 1978 (173).
From the Dartford (Kent) hoard of 1825.

'Sweting at Oxford'. The reverse die is a regular London product; Sweting had originally worked with two colleagues for Stephen. This coin was probably struck soon after the Battle of Lincoln in February, 1141, when Robert d'Oilly, castellan of Oxford, went over to the Empress.

19. :MA[TIL]LIS: IM[PE]R·
+WILEM:D[E:CA]ERDI· *cross botonnée on saltire fleury*
1.06 g. 45°. E.1000/67. From the Coed-y-Wenallt treasure trove, 1980.

This is a 'mule' linking the original Maudian issue (nos.9,15, same die) with a new reverse design, denominated Class B in the Wenallt report to avoid confusion with Stephen's Type II (no.38). The adoption of a new type is reasonably connected with the Maudian victory at Lincoln in February, 1141. Class B, however, was struck only at Cardiff and Bristol apart from Swansea (no.23) and no specimens have been found elsewhere. Stephen, too, had types which were of a local importance only — III, IV and V; his Type VI is not much commoner.

19

20

21

26

22

23

24

20. :IM[PE]ATRI · *(sic) crowned bust holding sceptre, right*
+ELWINE DE [CAIERDI] *cross botonnée on saltire fleury*
1.02 g. 90°. 94.40%. E.1000/72, From the Coed-y-Wenallt treasure trove, 1980.

This coin and the next betray the handiwork, for the new Class B, of a different die-sinker, coarse but neat in style. As on some other coins of the Empress, the Anglo-Norman preposition *de* is preferred to the Old English *on*. The moneyer, like 'Eini' at Swansea, is deceptively Welsh-looking; but it is Ælfwine, not Elwyn, in any case a modern name in Welsh.

21. IM · HE · MA · / +IOLI:DE:BRIT:C[AIE]R
1.06 g. 90°. E.1000/87. From the Coed-y-Wenallt treasure trove, 1980.

This astonishing obverse legend at first sight unites the names of the Empress and her son, or perhaps her father; but although there was ample room for it, there is no F (for *filius* or *filia*, according to which of the above suggestions is favoured), and in either case one would have expected the relationship to be indicated. In harmony with Maudian propaganda, however, HE is more likely to have stood for *heres*, 'heir', and the legend may be expanded *Imperatrix Heres Mathildis*, 'Maud the Empress, Heir (to the Kingdom)'. See no.31.

Joli the Norman incomer was still known by his place of origin, Breteuil (*de Britolio*). The 'customs' or charter under which this minor borough in Normandy flourished had an importance out of all proportion to its size, for these regulations were extended by rule-of-thumb Norman magnates to their boroughs in this country, and first of all to Hereford. Cardiff's charter contained some clauses going back to Breteuil, though as a whole it was modelled on that of Tewkesbury, which also belonged to the Consul.

The next seven coins bear other names, and include three in the name of Henry, attributed rightly or wrongly to Henry fitz Empress (nos.25-27).

22. IOHAN *crowned bust holding sceptre, right*
+WILLEM:DE[:]CAI[ERDI] *cross botonnée on saltire fleury*
0.95 g. 45°. E.1000/103. Stray from the Coed-y-Wenallt treasure trove; bought Spink, 1987.

Another obverse die, represented by a single specimen in the Wenallt hoard, reads · [IOH]AN IOHA and is also by the moneyer Willelm. A third fragmentary coin seems to begin its obverse inscription I[.....] and is by Willelm. Who was this John, and how came he to usurp the place of the royal name on these coins? There is contemporary warrant for coins struck by barons; of these one can rule out John the Marshal, John fitz Gilbert (who operated on the Maudian, and his own, account from nowhere nearer to Cardiff than Marlborough) on the basis of the second obverse given above. John *fitz* John is not attested, however likely a name in itself; but a John of *St.* John — St-Jean-le-Thomas in Normandy — was one of Robert fitz Haimo's fabled paladins who helped him win Glamorgan. That a member of the St. John family may be commemorated on these coins is exciting for all those interested in local history; but as there would be no record otherwise of the St. Johns in Glamorgan anything like as early as the 12th century, choice may perhaps fall on a John of St. John — *Johannes de Sancto Johanne* — who was a Maudian official in Oxfordshire, and who may have come to Glamorgan as steward during the Consul's imprisonment in September-November, 1141. As to why his name appeared instead of Maud's, see no.23.

23. +hENR[ICI]dE NOVOB
+HENRI:ON:S[W]EN
1.02 g. 180°. E.1000/98. From the Coed-y-Wenallt treasure trove, 1980.

Henry de Neubourg (the genitive of the Latinised form given on the coin, borne out by die-duplicates in the hoard — three in all — is probably derived from the inscription on his seal, which would have read *S(igillum) Henrici de Novo Burgo)* was mentioned under no.11. Under his command the Normans successfully expelled the Welsh from Gower. However, Henry was acting on behalf of Roger, second Earl of Warwick, their widowed mother, the Countess Margery, having been given Gower as her jointure in case of remarriage.

Once the Earl went over to the Maudian camp in 1140, Gower of necessity followed. Why, then, was the Empress's name not inscribed on the second (and last) issue of coins from the Swansea mint? The answer must be that they not only paralleled the new Class B of Cardiff mint in design, but were produced at exactly the same time as the issue of John of St. John (probably autumn 1141).

The retention of the royal bust with its symbolic crown and sceptre is the key to a proper understanding of the so-called baronial issues of this period. The hierarchical structure of society, and in particular of its nobility, ensured that these trappings were not lightly assumed. As Duke of Normandy, for example, William is shown with his sword-of-state in Tapestry scenes (cf.p.16); but King Edward, and in his turn Harold himself, are shown in kingly pose with crown and sceptre. Thus we may conclude that a distinction could be drawn between (a) the royal prerogative and nature of coinage in England; and (b) a need to express, in turbulent times, a local authority for the sometimes rather poorly-produced money, over and above that of the moneyer whose guarantee might so often be obscured (p.10). We may perhaps think of the baronial issues as essentially military. The appearance of their lord's name or that of his paymaster would have reassured mercenaries at a time when much base material was in circulation. But the great magnates, such as the Consul, left these matters to subordinates: 'Robert' coins there are, but not his.

24. +B · R · C · I · T · B · R · [..]: *crowned facing bust, pierced star on either side*
+BRIIT · P · ON · TO: *cross botonnée over concave quadrilateral*
1.05 g. 270°. E.975. Bought Baldwin, 1986 from Spink 6th Sale 1979 (520).

This unique coin was first published in 1889 without provenance. Much ingenuity has been lavished on the interpretation of its enigmatic legends. Two Maudian barons have been suggested as responsible for it — Baldwin de Redvers, Earl of Devon, in that case with Totnes as the place of mintage — it had had a mint as late as Henry I; and Brien fitz Count (son, that is, of Alain Count of Brittany, a favourite of Henry I): Brien was Lord of Wallingford, throughout the war the most easterly bastion of the Empress's cause, as well as Lord of Abergavenny in succession to Hamelin de Ballon, until 1141 when Maud granted it away to another favourite supporter, Milo of Gloucester, created Earl of Hereford; he died in 1143, leaving his son Roger as Earl (p.7).

Recent careful examination of the piece has rectified the readings on both sides. The second B and R are as certain as anything can be: that makes Brien fitz Count with equal certainty the issuer. Of the two final letters nothing definite can be said, for of them only an upright shows of the second; but it is reasonable to think that one of them was an F. The obverse would then read *Br(ienus): C(om)it(is) Bri(ttanie) F(ilius)* or *Br(ittanie) Fi(lius)*, preferably the former; 'Brien son of the Count of Brittany'. The reverse seems to embody a moneyer *Brihtwi*

25

26

27

28

29

30

(Beorhtwine) *'on To——'*, which cannot of course be Totnes now, but possibly 'at *Tor*', 'at the Tower' in reference to Wallingford Castle, of which the great mound still remains: the borough mint, inactive since Henry I, would have 'signed' PEL, WAL, etc.

* * * * *

We come now to the pennies which have been attributed to Henry fitz Empress. Others bearing his name and the title *Rex*, while of the same period, cannot possibly be his, because he was not king then. There is some doubt as to whether any coins were struck in his name. Roger de Hoveden writes that in 1149 Henry instituted a coinage while he was in England, which was called 'Duke's money', and that he suppressed private issues. But Henry was not then Duke of Normandy or Aquitaine; and Ralph de Diceto tells us, on the contrary, that a uniform coinage was to be provided under the terms of the treaty of 1153. This is Stephen's Type VII (no.39). Roger de Hoveden seems to have telescoped the two visits. The status of the next three coins is uncertain. Some would explain all coins naming a Henry — or a William for that matter (no.28) — as the work of moneyers playing safe and naming past kings. In that case one may wonder why obsolete designs were not more exactly followed.

25. *[+hE]NRICV[S] crowned facing bust, pierced star on either side*
[+]AREFIN:ON:BRIC cross botonnée over concave quadrilateral
1.03 g. 315°. E.985. Bought Norweb I Sale, 1985 (120).

Arnfinnr coined at Bristol for the Empress, and Bristol was the greatest of all her strongholds. An issue in the name of her son, either in 1149 when he came over to be knighted at Carlisle, or in 1153, is not improbable. The design of this coin, like the preceding one and also no.28, is closely based on William I's Type V, with stars for Normandy and England. Three examples of the present coin are recorded, all from the same reverse die; one in the Royal Danish Collection has been in Copenhagen since the 1740's, as Dr Jensen of that cabinet has informed the writer: they can hardly be false.

William I Type V, moneyer Leofwine at Bristol. E.757.

26. *hENRICV · S h crowned bust holding sceptre, right*
+P[I]LLELM ON:C · R · S : T cross fleury on quadrilateral fleury
0.95 g. 360°. E.986. Bought Baldwin, 1986, from .... Hollis Sale, 1817 (176).

This unique piece exhibits a Stephen Type I obverse design and a Henry I Type XV reverse. The C in the name has been cut as E, the S is on its side; and the final letter seems to be an uncial *h*, which may stand for *heres* as on nos. 21 and 31; in that case the Henry named would indeed be Henry fitz Empress, *'rectus heres Angliae'* — 'right heir of England' as he is denominated in certain charters. The mint is colourably explained as *C(i)r(ece)st(re)*, Cirencester, an important Maudian stronghold from 1142. Moneyer and mint are shared with another coin having an obverse in the name of a William, possibly William Earl of Gloucester from 1147, though his father never struck coins in his own name.

Henry I Type XV, moneyer Saeric at Hereford. E.851.

27.   hENRICVS h
+[PIHCRI]C:[O]N:hER
1.01 g. 270°. E.987. Bought Norweb IV Sale, 1987 (1287). From ... Bergne Sale, 1873 (328).

The Type I obverse is close in style to another represented by two coins in the British Museum with Type I reverse. Here the terminal *h* in the obverse legend is damaged by double-striking, and uncertain. Wihtric we met on no.6. Henry was here at Hereford in 1149, when he joined Earl Roger to go to Carlisle where they were knighted, and where they plotted the seizure of York. Nos.25 and 27 are so different that it is difficult to believe that they were struck on the same visit to England.

28.   [+]WI[LL]ELMVS *crowned bust facing, pierced star to either side*
+[RO]GIER:D[E:P]AR *voided cross botonnée over concave quadrilateral*
0.97 g. 315°. E.988 Bought Norweb IV Sale, 1987 (1288).

This coin was first published with no.24 and likewise without provenance, but a second specimen from the same dies is recorded. The identity of the William named on this Wareham penny by Stephen's Type I moneyer there, Rodger, is obscure. Stephen's younger son can be ruled out; and if William de Mohun, Earl of Dorset & Somerset was meant, the coin must have been struck at farthest before 1144, when his loyalty to Maud had faded. It is possible that William, Earl of Gloucester in succession to the Consul in 1147 is intended; he may have provided some assistance to Henry fitz Empress in the latter stages of his visit to England as a rather troublesome adolescent in that year, or possibly in 1149; but his father had never struck coins in his own name. Given the importance of Wareham as a port of embarkation and entry, the moneyer may have taken refuge in reviving William I's Type V as an evasion. If so the choice was curious, though the likeliest and latest of the Conqueror's types, the ubiquitous PAXS penny, is so common today mainly because of the Beauworth hoard of 1833 (p.11).

ROYALIST COINS

There was a desperate need for cash to finance countermeasures against the triumphant Maudians after Stephen's capture in February 1141, and in this connexion a curious series of pennies of a possible Flemish affinity attracts notice, though a later date in the decade may equally well account for them or some of them. They are well-represented in the Museum's collection (nos.33-37). Other coins also illustrate the period (nos.29-32). Some time after the king's release, a new type was produced for him at some seventeen mints in the eastern half of the kingdom, his Type II (no.38; see the map).

29.   +STIEFNE:R *crowned bust holding sceptre, right; a crescent between nose and sceptre.*
+ALVRE[D D]E LVNDEN *cross moline and lilies*
1.43 g. 45°. E.925. Bought Baldwin, 1986, from the North Collection ... and Grantley IV Sale, 1944 (1291).

The London moneyer is Alfred, who struck Type I and the Peréric coinage (no.10); the style of this piece owes little to the prewar fitz Otto workshop. In later heraldry, a crescent was the accepted

31

32

33

34

35

36

standard mark of cadency for a second son, but that was not the position as early as the 1140's. The crescent, however, was already associated with the House of Boulogne, whose active daughter was Stephen's Queen Matilda, untiring in her efforts to set him free. This must be a coin of that period. No exploitation of equal cogency can be proposed for the small devices which appear, e.g. on nos.3, 11 or 23, which seem to be merely added to identify particular dies or the coins struck from them, as a means of control.

30. +STEPHANVS REX *crowned bust holding sceptre, right*
+WALCHELINVS [D]ERBI *voided cross, eagles in spandrels*
1.33 g., pierced. 270°. E.961. Bought Baldwin, 1978, from the Hanham collection .... and Marsham Sale, 1888 (267).

This is one of ten from the same pair of dies, locally cut. Walchelin is otherwise known in connexion with Derby, where this coin was probably struck during the king's captivity, or shortly afterwards, on the authority of Robert II de Ferrers, Earl of Derby and Nottinghamshire, a stout supporter of the king until 1148, when he became for several years an ally of Ranulf, Earl of Chester and so a Maudian. The Latin form of the king's name is probably derived from a seal or charter. The reverse imitates a distinctive type of Edward the Confessor, current over 80 years before; perhaps one had come to light and was thought handsome enough to copy, or perhaps (as Marion Archibald has suggested) the eagles were taken to be falcons (*falchuns* in Anglo-Norman) and employed as an approximate play on the name of the moneyer.

31. +RODB Ð ST · hE *outwardly; crowned bust holding sceptre, right*
+WI · S · Ð · GNOTIA *cross moline and lilies*
1.12 g. 90°. E.973. Bought Spink, 1984, from the Mack collection (but not in the Mack Sylloge SCBI, *vol.20). Found near Peterborough, 1932.*

Edward the Confessor Type IX, moneyer Leofwine at Gloucester. E.657.

The writer reads the obverse of this unique penny *Rodb(ertus de St(utevilla) H(eres)*, 'Robert de Stuteville the Heir', and the reverse — questionably — as *Wi(llemu)s de Gnotia*, 'William of [?] *Gernetteby* (Carnaby)', near York, whose later namesake witnessed a Stuteville charter (for this was their region) about 1201; William also struck a penny in Stephen's name of very similar style, as well as one with illiterate obverse and reverse interspersed with ornaments. Robert de Stuteville was landless; his grandfather had forfeited extensive holdings in England as a supporter of Robert, Duke of Normandy, and was captured with him at the battle of Tinchebray in 1106. It will be remembered that Duke Robert ended his perpetual imprisonment at Cardiff Castle, where the Consul was responsible for him, in 1134; Robert I de Stuteville was also condemned to life imprisonment, and the Normandy holdings passed to his son and our Robert's elder brother.

Robert III de Stuteville probably came to England in Stephen's entourage in 1137, and played a part at the Battle of the Standard near Northallerton in 1138. In a charter he refers to *hereditas mea*, which he was seeking to recover in full from the Crown and from the Mowbray family who had been granted part. As a loyal supporter of Stephen, he would have become a focal point of royalist endeavour after Lincoln; see p. 28 for the significance of a subject's name on coins of this period.

32. +S[TEFNE · R]EX: *crowned bust holding sceptre, right; no inner circle*
+SANSON[:ON ANT] *voided cross moline and lilies*
1.04 g. 90°. E.960. Bought Spink, 1983.

'Sanson at *(H)antune* (Southampton)'. The moneyer was perhaps a Jewish merchant, though Southampton — so-called to distinguish it from Northampton — was of small importance at this period. Several minor varieties of this penny are known; it is associated in the Linton (Maidstone) hoard with Stephen's Type II, and in the Awbridge (Hants.) hoard with Type VII. These associations enable it to be assigned to the mid or late 1140's; one might have expected a Type II issue instead of this variant of Type I, but the nearest Type II mints are fairly distant at Lewes and Dorchester (Oxon.).

* * * * *

Nos. 33-37 belong to the group with apparent Flemish affinities. Their style is un-English and their legends are interspersed with, or replaced by, ornaments. The guarantee of moneyer's name plus place of mintage has gone: William 'of Carnaby'(?) and a known sheriff or *ealdormann* of York, Thomas fitz Ulviet, are personal names that we can recognise, but occur without a mint-name; and *Eboracum* (York) is spelt out in full (or sometimes very abbreviated form, as on no.33) on other coins without personal name. On this basis the series has been dubbed the 'York Group'; and that its centre was York is borne out by the discovery at Cattal, 13 miles to the west, of a substantial find as long ago as 1684. Nearly all known specimens may emanate from this hoard, for York Group pennies did not enter normal circulation — none in the Prestwich (Manchester) hoard of 1972, with its worn Type I's — and must have served some special purpose: pay for the Flemish mercenaries who formed the backbone of the royal army is a likely one.

Saint-Omer. Petits deniers, mid to late 12th century. After Poey d'Avant.

Peter Seaby has looked to western Flanders for the source of designs and has questioned whether the coins need be English. Particularly interesting is his recognition of the letters S and (rounded) M amid ornaments and other letters on the reverse of some specimens (no.33), for the same letters are found on coins struck at Saint-Omer. However, the York Group pieces look just as out-of-place among Flemish issues of the period and have never been claimed as other than English by continental scholars. It is uncertain when Saint-Omer began the use of these two letters as indicated; and if the coins are English then it is difficult to see how Saint-Omer, well beyond the borders of Stephen's County of Boulogne, can have come into the picture. The only likely link seems to be through William of Ypres, a younger son of the Count of Flanders and a mercenary chief of the deepest dye,

37

38

39

40

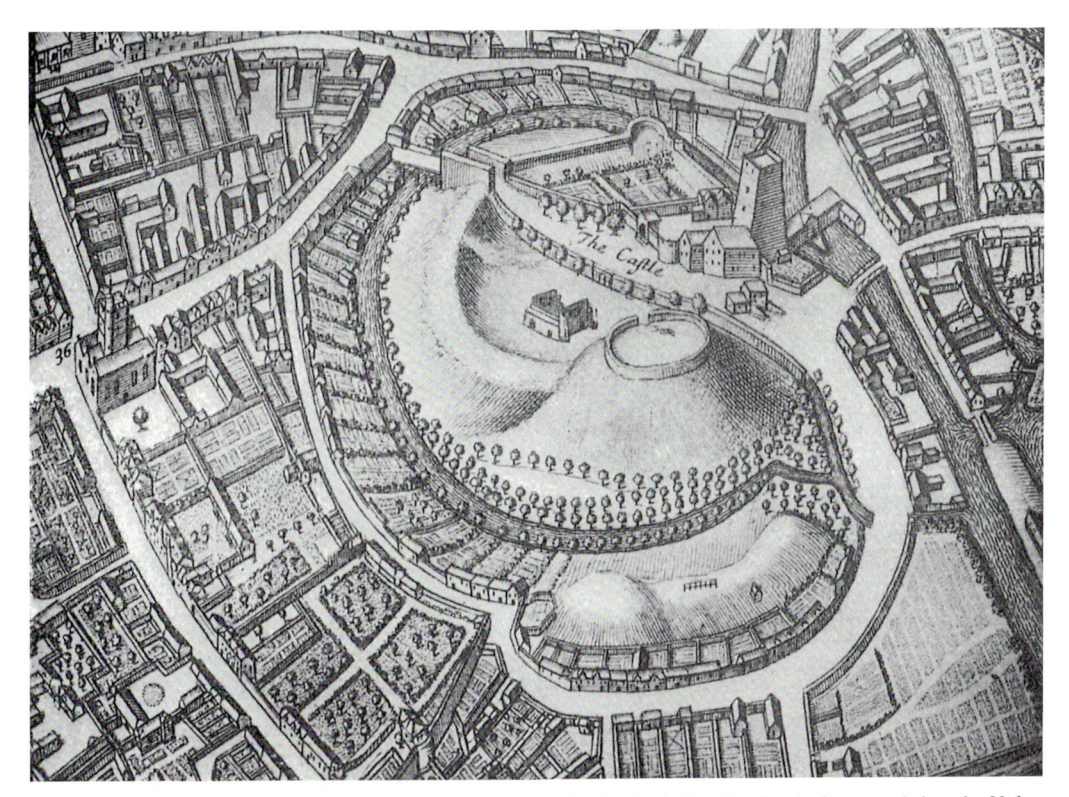

Oxford Castle after the demolition of 1649, already surrounded by the developing city. In the foreground rises the 60 ft. castle-mound, with the remains of a shell-keep on top, as at Cardiff. To left, the bailey curves round to a bridge over the moat; the wall and towers on top of the earthwork have gone, but survive in part beyond the bridge. The very tall tapering tower was probably the residence of the Empress Maud during the winter siege of 1142 (p.7). This tower still stands, as does the mound. From Loggan's Oxonia Illustrata, *1675.*

early recruited by Stephen and taken into his confidence; he was destined, after the successful routing of the Empress's army in 1141, to be the Consul's gaoler at Rochester Castle. He is not known to have had any York connexion; but Stephen marched to York in order to confront the advancing forces of Henry fitz Empress in 1149, so that the coinage may be a reflection of the preparations made at this time, and the product of a Flemish die-sinker. One clue to the date is the identity of the Eustace named with Eustace fitz John, for he is so named on a unique fragmentary penny in the British Museum of his 'lion' type (cf.no.37). He was a staunch supporter of the Empress, having fought with the Scots at Northallerton in 1138; but by 1146 he had turned his coat. He will not have done so, however, as early as 1141, when the Empress's star was at its zenith; and it must seem, accordingly, that the Eustace pieces are towards the end of a series which might very well have begun during the king's captivity with a coin of strongly political content, such as no.35.

33. +STIENE R *crowned bust holding lance-flag, right; star under.*
E ω S L A ω B S *backwards, interspaced with ornaments; cross moline and lilies*
1.00 g. 315°. E.962. Bought Baldwin, 1978, from the Hanham coll. and ... Drabble Sale, 1939 (730).

Note EB for Eboracum and the S and rounded M which have been linked with Saint-Omer. About 17 'flag' pennies are known, including a cut halfpenny from Yarm, near Darlington. The obverse is slightly double-struck on this example.

The lance-flag (*gonfanon*) taking the place of the sceptre was the mark of a knight and leader of men; they appear on the Bayeux Tapestry, on seals, and on coins, notably the thin, one-sided *pfennige* of eastern Germany (p.42). These pennons were coloured and might carry a cross or other device,

but as with the devices on the shields, one is only at the dawn of heraldry (Geoffrey of Anjou was given, when knighted by Henry I in 1127, a shield with golden lioncels upon it, and is shown with it on the mortuary enamel plaque at Le Mans. That is regarded as the earliest acceptable instance of personal bearings, and the lioncels certainly went down in the family). The coin was probably inspired by Stephen's second seal, adopted in June, 1139, whereon his mounted figure carries a gonfanon; the penny cannot well be earlier, for ordinary Type I was struck at York. There can thus be no connexion with the great conjoint standard of SS. Peter of York, John of Beverley and Wilfred of Ripon wheeled on to the battlefield at Northallerton in 1138, which gave its name to that battle *'de Standardo'*.

Impression of the obverse of Stephen's second seal. Full size. After Trésor de Numismatique et de Glyptique, *1835.*

34. *[+S]TIEN and ornaments; crowned bust holding sceptre, right.*
Ornaments; cross pattée over saltire fleury
1.01 g. 45°. E.964. Bought Spink, 1986. Said to have been found near Grimsby (? with other coins).

Three of this type, from the same dies, are known. The spelling of the name may reflect a French influence, *(E)stien*, interesting in that the sceptre, as Peter Seaby has pointed out, is of a French pattern first seen on the seal of Louis VII (1137-80); it appears also on those of his two successors. The normal lily at the tip is replaced by an open lozenge containing a very small lily (a rosette on the coins). On the English coin it may have reminded people that not only had Stephen done homage to the French king (then Louis VI) for Normandy as a fief of the French Crown, but had married his son Eustace to Louis VII's own sister. It may hint at the prospect of powerful support for the discomfited royalist cause, and suggest 1141 as the date of the coin.

Impression of the obverse of Philip Augustus' seal, 1180-1223, with lozengular-tipped sceptre. Full size. After Trésor de Numismatique et de Glyptique, *1834.*

35. *+STIEFNE R two standing figures facing each other; a tall lily-sceptre between them*
S, among ornaments; cross fleury on saltire botonnée
1.34 g. 180°. E.963. Bought Baldwin, 1978, from the Hanham coll. and ... Drabble Sale, 1939 (734).

Edward Hawkins in 1841 was the first to point out that the artist had attempted 'to indicate the female form' in the shorter figure on the right — with its long hair and undivided lower garment quite different from the left-hand, taller figure. Scholars have accepted his suggestion that the coin represents Queen Matilda's support for her husband during his captivity in 1141. The two-figure type, derived from Byzantine models, appears here and there in early medieval Europe. A *pfennig* of Albert 'the Bear', Margrave of Brandenburg 1134-70, is particularly handsome and shows the Margravine Sophia standing beside him; both wear ermine mantles. A Flemish *petit denier* and derivatives, of a type introduced *c.*1140, may copy our piece, which to judge by 17 surviving examples from several dies must have belonged to a considerable issue. Certain pennies of the Confessor (Type IX, p.36) show him seated holding orb and *long* sceptre, the only other occurrence of this in our coinage. As to attire, Stephen is represented as wearing a long mail hauberk deeply divided and back, thus giving the deceptive appearance of trousers (which would have been very uncomfortable!). The conical helmet with its nose-piece is laced on to the mail hood, and here we see just the laces at the back; like the rich helmets described in the *Chanson de Roland* (written

Pfennig of Albert 'the Bear', Margrave of Brandenburg 1134-70. After Koehne, 1843.

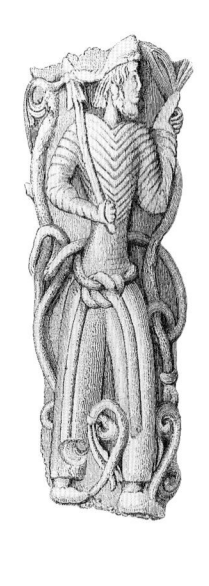

Stylized knights wearing long hauberks divided front and back, giving the effect of trousers. 12th century, S.portal of Kilpeck church, Hereford. After Basire, 1843. By permission of the Society of Antiquaries.

down in England towards 1100), we may imagine it as being of gold set with gems. Over all, Stephen wears a long mantle, as also does the queen over a long robe with the fashionable trailing sleeves of the time; on her head is a diadem which confines the kerchief worn by all respectable women in deference to the dictate of St.Paul; it is the floating ends of this, and *not* loose tresses, which Hawkins observed (back cover).

36. *[+]RODBERTVS D[E STV] mounted knight [brandishing sword], right*
D, among ornaments; cross pattée over saltire fleury
0.96 g., chipped. 360°. E.974. Bought Baldwin, 1986, from ... the Pembroke Sale, 1848 (59) — a collection closed since 1733. Probably from the Cattal hoard, 1684. Illustrated by Ducarel in 1757.

Three of the four known examples are from the same dies, but only one (in Glasgow) has the complete legend. Here we see Robert de Stuteville III (cf.no.31), drawn probably from his seal. The protection of the divided hauberk is very clear. The helmet has extra reinforcements front and back. Perhaps Robert commanded a band of Flemish mercenaries. The date of the coin must lie before the introduction of Stephen's regular Type VI at York, at furthest towards 1150.

37. *+EISTAOhIVS: lion passant right, recurved tail; ornaments*
Ornaments; cross pattée over saltire fleury
0.93 g., chipped 315°? E.970. Bought Baldwin, 1978 from ... Drabble Sale, 1939 (732). Probably from the Cattal hoard, 1684.

O for C in this problem piece, of which 20 are known, 19 from the same dies. Another type shows Eustace as a bearded knight on foot. Stephen's elder son has sometimes been claimed as the Eustace concerned; but he will not have been knighted until at least 1147 and had nothing to do with York, though the same may be said of a

Henricus Episcopus, whose royal connexion is shown by his crown — the king's brother, in effect — mentioned on another coin still. But the full legend quoted above (p.40) is not to be dismissed lightly, despite the obscurity surrounding Eustace fitz John's activities in the earlier 1140's. His base was at Malton. Later he became Constable of Chester, and died in an ambush at Basingwerk during Henry II's Welsh expedition of 1157 against Owain Gwynedd.

38. *[+STI]EFNE facing crowned bust holding sceptre +R[ODBER]T:O[N:]LVN voided cross botonnée, pierced stars in spandrels*
1.41 g. 360°. E.909. Bought Baldwin, 1978.

'Rodbert at London'. It would not be proper to close the wartime series without including as a tail-piece a typical example of Stephen's Type II, struck in seventeen mints in southern and eastern England where the king retained full control, and in distant Durham where the Bishop favoured him. We notice that the arched crown with pendants is again being worn. The dating of the type is imprecise. A new issue after Stephen's release would have been desirable for fiscal reasons (p. 11), but some scholars would postpone the appearance of Type II until nearly the end of the decade. All things considered, *c.*1145-50 seems likely, and allows Type VI — from only eight mints all within the shadow of Type II — to be struck close to 1153. The dating of Types III, IV and V, which are very rare, and indeed local, is likewise uncertain.

The End of the Tale

As already explained (p.32), the *moneta Ducis* was a misnomer for Stephen's final Type VII (no.39), for under the Treaty of Westminster in 1153 Stephen reserved the exercise of justice, which indeed he could not delegate, however much he otherwise undertook to defer to Henry's advice. The coinage was part of the king's prerogative also. Type VII was therefore issued in Stephen's name by some 38 mints (black circles on the map), including Gloucester and Hereford, but eschewing in the most pointed manner Bristol, Cardiff, Wareham and Oxford where coins in Maud's name had been struck; Bath, almost as pointedly, was resuscitated instead. Bristol, Oxford and for that matter Wallingford were reprieved by Henry II when the time came to change the coinage in 1158 (no.40). Pembroke then functioned afresh, but neither Swansea nor Cardiff was ever again the seat of a mint.

39. +STIEFNE · *crowned bust holding sceptre, threequarters left*
+PI[LLEM:ON:G]LOECE *voided cross within a quatrefoil with lilies at the angles*
1.33 g. 90°. E.919. Bought Elmore Jones II Sale, 1984 (1398).

'Willem at *Gloecestre* (Gloucester)'. The London die-cutting centre was again operating, though its personnel seems to have been rather inferior. The portrait is bearded, an interesting detail not previously known on the Norman coinage; the pose, otherwise, has affinities with Henry I's final Type XV — a pathetic choice, for Stephen lived barely another year. The coinage continued unchanged, however, until Henry II ordered new designs in 1158.

40. [+]hENRI[:R]E· *crowned bust holding sceptre, quarter left*
+W[IL]LAM:ON:CAR: *cross pattée, crosslets in spandrels*
1.44 g. 225°. E.1015. Bought Baldwin, 1978.

'Willelm at Carlisle' — *not* Cardiff — the moneyer was the son of the Herebald who coined there for Stephen and then for the King of Scots and the Earl of Northumbria (no.12), his son. The weight of the penny is up: in 1158, Henry II ordered 20, rather than 21, to be struck from the 5,400 grain 'Tower' pound in use, in order to renew confidence in the currency. The roundness and also the rather light impression are typical of Carlisle at this period, and point to some refinement of the normal crude technique. The silver used here was local, the moneyer being also lessee of the Alston mines.

*****

In 1136, David King of Scots had captured Carlisle; in 1149 he had knighted Henry fitz Empress there; in 1153 he died there: it had been his favourite residence. His grandson Malcolm succeeded him, because Henry of Northumbria had also died; in 1157, Malcolm did homage to Henry as Earl of Huntingdon; the city and the north of England were restored. In January 1158, Henry paid a triumphal visit to Carlisle.

This penny is shown by certain details to be a few years later than that visit. On it, Henry is shown wearing what is thought to be the massive lily-crown used at his coronation. It has an interesting history, having belonged to his mother's first husband, the Emperor Henry V. Stephen of

Rouen tells us as much in a list appended to his poem *Draco Normannicus* ('The Norman Dragon'), for it was part of the amazing treasure given by the Empress to the Abbey of Bec when she was gravely ill after Henry's birth and was not expected to live. The crown was set with precious stones and had removeable arches and terminal cross of solid gold (quite rightly not shown on the coins, arches making an imperial crown, strictly speaking), and was so heavy that it required to be supported by attendants, silver rings being provided for that purpose.

Further Reading

R.H.C. Davies, *King Stephen* (1967 and reprinted since) — the best narrative.

Nesta Pain, *Empress Matilda* (1978) — a good biography.

R.P. Mack, 'Stephen and the Anarchy 1135-1154' in *The British Numismatic Journal*, vol. xxxv, 1966, pp.38-112, 12 pls., provides a comprehensive listing, but is out-of-date in some statements.

G.C. Boon, *Welsh Hoards 1979-1981* (National Museum of Wales, 1986), pp.37-82, describes the Wenallt hoard and its setting in detail.

B.A. Seaby Ltd., *Standard Catalogue of British Coins*, i: *Coins of England and the United Kingdom,* published annually, is a well-illustrated handbook where all the Types mentioned here will be found.

C.H.V. Sutherland, *English Coinage* (1973), and Peter Seaby, *The Story of British Coinage* (1985), are the most recent general surveys.